Brands We Know

Hot Wheels

By Sara Green

Bellwether Media • Minneapolis, MN

Jump into the cockpit and take flight with *Pilot* books. Your journey will take you on high-energy adventures as you learn about all that is wild, weird, fascinating, and fun!

This edition first published in 2017 by Bellwether Media, Inc.

Library of Congress Cataloging-in-Publication Data

Names: Green, Sara, 1964- author.
Title: Hot Wheels / by Sara Green.
Description: Minneapolis, MN : Bellwether Media, Inc., 2017. | Series: Pilot:
   Brands We Know | Includes bibliographical references and index.
Identifiers: LCCN 2016034524 (print) | LCCN 2016035177 (ebook) | ISBN
   9781626175556 (hardcover : alk. paper) |
ISBN 9781681033020 (ebook)
Subjects: LCSH: Hot Wheels toys--Juvenile literature.
Classification: LCC TL237 .G695 2017 (print) | LCC TL237 (ebook)
   | DDC 629.22/1--dc23
LC record available at https://lccn.loc.gov/2016034524

Editor: Christina Leighton   Designer: Josh Brink

Printed in the United States of America, North Mankato, MN.

Table of Contents

What Is the Hot Wheels Brand?

Two toy sports cars, a Ford and a Mazda, are lined up at the starting gate. They wait at the top of a steep orange track. These are not ordinary toys. They are Hot Wheels! A push of a button launches the cars down the track. They loop the loop and zip across tilted curves. Suddenly, the Ford flies off the track. The Mazda wins! Is it the fastest car or just lucky? Another race is on!

Hot Wheels is a **brand** of **die-cast** toy cars. A large toy company called Mattel, Inc. makes them. Mattel's **headquarters** is in El Segundo, California. The Hot Wheels brand includes cars, vans, trucks, and other vehicles. Track sets and playsets are top sellers. Hot Wheels **collectibles** are also popular. The brand's red and yellow flame **logo** is even found on some real race cars. Today, Hot Wheels outnumber all the real cars in the world!

By the Numbers

more than
4 billion
Hot Wheels vehicles
made since 1968

332 feet
(101 meters) jumped by Hot Wheels
driver Tanner Foust in 2011

more than
$1 million
spent on some Hot
Wheels collections

$72,000
paid for a pink
1969 Volkswagen
Beach Bomb

8
Hot Wheels cars sold
every second

Launching Hot Wheels

A man named Elliot Handler created Hot Wheels in 1968. Elliot had created the Mattel company with his wife, Ruth, more than twenty years earlier. Elliot wanted to make a special toy for boys after Mattel's success with Barbie dolls for girls. He hired professional car designers to help make Hot Wheels.

In 1968, Mattel introduced 16 toy cars. Each one was based on an actual car. They looked different from other toy cars on store shelves. Hot Wheels cars were painted in bright **Spectraflame** colors and came with red-rimmed tires. Their **axles** and plastic wheels helped them roll faster than other toy cars. Small details, such as side **exhaust** pipes, made them look like real cars. Kids loved their sporty looks and fast speeds. The cars sold for 59 cents each and included a metal collector's button. In the first year, Mattel sold more than 16 million cars. Hot Wheels toys were huge!

Elliot Handler

Rocket Science
A missile engineer named Jack Ryan was one of the first Hot Wheels designers. His knowledge helped the team create cars that reached high speeds.

Original 16 from 1968

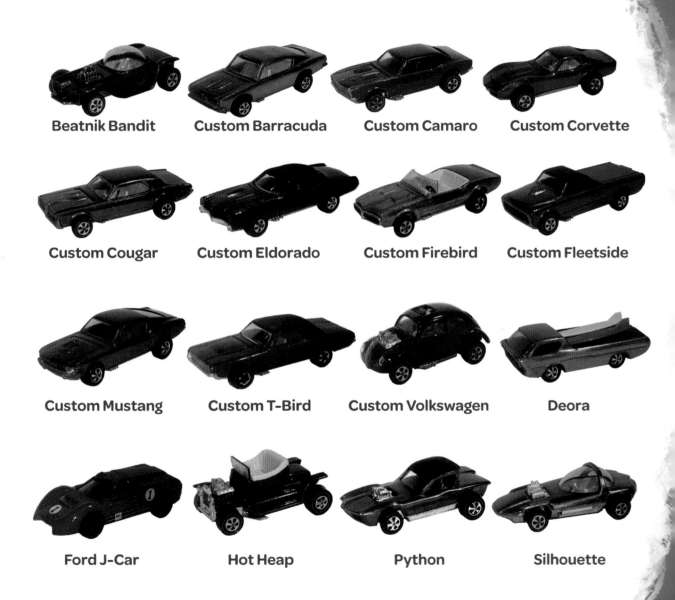

Beatnik Bandit

Custom Barracuda

Custom Camaro

Custom Corvette

Custom Cougar

Custom Eldorado

Custom Firebird

Custom Fleetside

Custom Mustang

Custom T-Bird

Custom Volkswagen

Deora

Ford J-Car

Hot Heap

Python

Silhouette

Fastest Metal Cars in the World!

1960s tagline

The Collection Grows

Demand for Hot Wheels exploded. Elliot and his team worked quickly to design more cars. They added 24 Hot Wheels cars in 1969. The group included two original cars called the Twin Mill and Splittin' Image. The Snake and Mongoose funny cars were introduced in 1970. Their bodies flipped up to reveal the engines inside. A drag race set with these cars was hugely popular. Kids loved pitting the two cars against each other! Cars called Sizzlers also came on the market in 1970. These cars had a built-in motor and a tiny battery.

Snake and Mongoose re-creation cars

During this time, Hot Wheels boosted its **advertising**. A popular Saturday morning cartoon series based on the toys began in 1969. It featured a sports car called Jack Rabbit Special. This car was also part of the 1970 Hot Wheels line. For a while, Shell gas stations offered a Hot Wheels car with each fill. Jack in the Box restaurants also gave a free Hot Wheels car to customers.

Over time, the variety of Hot Wheels cars grew. Mattel began experimenting with different paint styles in the 1970s, including **fluorescent** colors. The company stopped using Spectraflame paint in 1973. It was replaced with a paint called **enamel**. The tires also changed. By the late 1970s, Mattel stopped painting red lines on Hot Wheels tires.

Redlines
Original Hot Wheels with red around their tires are extremely popular collector's items. They are often called Redlines.

Go with the Winner
1970s tagline

Cool Collections
Many people enjoy collecting Hot Wheels. Some collections are worth more than $1 million!

New Hot Wheels lines **debuted** in the 1980s. The Hot Ones had thinner axles for more speed. Many had painted gold **hubs**. Real Riders were also introduced during this time. They had rubber tires that looked and felt real. Kids could take them off and put them back on. The rubber tires made Real Riders slower than other Hot Wheels. However, the cars were still popular. HiRakers also came on the market in the 1980s. Their rear wheels could be raised and lowered. Many fans liked this cool feature!

Real Rider

A popular series called Treasure Hunt debuted in the 1990s. The cars are less common than other Hot Wheels. Today, Treasure Hunt cars are hidden within other series. A small flame symbol on cars identifies them, but finding them can be a challenge! The even more rare Super Treasure Hunts were introduced in 2007. They have a new type of Spectraflame paint and Real Rider tires. A "TH" symbol is found somewhere on the car. Super Treasure Hunts are also hidden within other series. It takes sharp eyes to spot them!

'59 Chevy Delivery from 2011

Treasure Hunts

Another popular line called Faster Than Ever was first released in 2005. The axles on the wheels were coated with nickel to reduce **friction**. The wheels had open holes and five spokes. This design looked flashy and helped increase speeds.

Almost too real
2000s tagline

Faster Than Ever

13

Fast Tracks

Hot Wheels racing is extra fun with track sets! These plastic tracks have been popular since the early days of the brand. Bright orange is the most recognized track color. Tracks come in sections so they can be built in many ways. Short, straight tracks are great for quick races. Longer racetracks often have loops, ramps, and tilted curves.

A Giant Double Dare Snare

In 2012, two drivers successfully finished a life-sized Hot Wheels Double Dare Snare track!

Track sets also have a variety of **accessories**. Launchers make cars fly down the tracks. Power boosters use motors to add extra speed to cars. Kids can also challenge their cars to jump gaps and do other tricks. For these, speed is important or cars will fall to the ground. Some tracks are set up for crashes. Cars must launch exactly right to get through the crash zone!

Hot Wheels Today

Today's Hot Wheels come in even more styles and looks. Corvette and Mustang cars are ready to race as part of the Hot Wheels Race Team. The Street Beasts look like sharks, dragons, and other fierce creatures. Glow-in-the-dark cars are part of the Glow Wheels line. Color Shifters change colors when they are dunked in hot or cold water. Extra flashy Art Cars and shiny Super Chromes are other popular lines. Hot Wheels also makes larger toy cars about 11 inches (28 centimeters) long. They have more details, such as seat belts and doors that open and close.

Art Cars

Street Beasts

THE BEATLES YELLOW SUBMARINE

The Beatles Yellow Submarine

A Prized Color

The first hot pink Hot Wheels cars were meant for girls. Today, hot pink is the rarest and most valuable Hot Wheels color!

1992 VW Golf

Make It Epic!

2010s tagline

2009 Killer Copter

The Hot Wheels brand offers more than cars. It also includes motorcycles, helicopters, planes, and even a yellow submarine. **Animated** movies bring Hot Wheels toys to life. Kids take the driver's seat playing Hot Wheels racing games. Other Hot Wheels games give an inside look at how cars are tested. Games may also teach ways to build bridges, tunnels, and tracks that float on water.

Outside the Track

Hot Wheels cars and tracks are not just toys. Some teachers use a Hot Wheels program called Speedometry to teach math and science to students. One lesson has students build the best ramps for speed. Another helps them discover how speed affects car crashes. These lessons teach kids about energy, force, and motion. They also help kids learn to work well in teams.

Hot Wheels also builds life-sized cars. These include real versions of the Twin Mill, Deora II, and Snake funny car. Hot Wheels transformed a Corvette into the powerful black Darth Vader Car. People can view life-sized Hot Wheels cars and race toy ones at the Hot Wheels Garage in El Segundo, California. This garage collects money to support **charities**.

Fans of all ages gather at **conventions** to see new Hot Wheels products and meet designers. Other activities include building custom cars and racing on track sets. Hot Wheels brings kids and adults together!

life-sized Hot Wheels Darth Vader Car

Hot Wheels Timeline

1968

Mattel makes a line of
16 die-cast
toy cars

1997

Hot Wheels and
NASCAR driver Kyle
Petty team up

1970

Snake and
Mongoose funny
cars hit shelves

1983

The Real Riders line is
introduced

1973

Enamel paint replaces
Spectraflame paint

1995

Treasure Hunts debut

1969

A line of 24 new
cars is released

2005
The Faster Than Ever
line is released

2016
Super Mario Hot
Wheels cars come out

2013
Hot Wheels starts
developing Speedometry

2012
Hot Wheels Wall Tracks
wins Boy Toy of the Year
and Innovative Toy of the
Year awards from the Toy
Industry Association

2007
Super Treasure Hunts
are introduced

2014
Hot Wheels makes
a life-sized Darth
Vader Car for the San
Diego Comic-Con

2003
The first animated
Hot Wheels movie,
*Hot Wheels World
Race*, is released

Glossary

accessories—things added to something else to make it more useful or attractive

advertising—using notices and messages to announce or promote something

animated—produced by the creation of a series of drawings that are shown quickly, one after the other, to give the appearance of movement

axles—bars on which wheels turn

brand—a category of products all made by the same company

charities—organizations that help others in need

collectibles—items valued and collected by people to keep or sell

conventions—meetings for people who share a common interest

debuted—were introduced for the first time

die-cast—formed by pouring liquid metal into a mold

enamel—a glossy, decorative coating

exhaust—the gas that leaves an engine

fluorescent—very bright

friction—the force caused by one object or surface rubbing against another

headquarters—a company's main office

hubs—the centers of wheels

logo—a symbol or design that identifies a brand or product

Spectraflame—a type of paint used on the bodies of cars to make them shine

To Learn More

AT THE LIBRARY

Gifford, Clive. *Car Crazy*. New York, N.Y.: DK Publishing, 2012.

McCollum, Sean. *Custom Cars: The Ins and Outs of Tuners, Hot Rods, and Other Muscle Cars*. Mankato, Minn.: Capstone Press, 2010.

Van Bogart, Angelo. *Hot Wheels: 40 Years*. Iola, Wisc.: Krause Publications, 2007.

ON THE WEB

Learning more about Hot Wheels is as easy as 1, 2, 3.

1. Go to www.factsurfer.com.

2. Enter "Hot Wheels" into the search box.

3. Click the "Surf" button and you will see a list of related web sites.

With factsurfer.com, finding more information is just a click away.

Index